## Make Your Own Art

# Painting

Sally Henry

RIVER FOREST P.L.

PowerKiDS
press

New York

Published in 2009 by The Rosen Publishing Group, Inc.
29 East 21st Street, New York, NY 10010

Editor: Alex Woolf
Designers: Sally Henry and Trevor Cook
Consultant: Daisy Fearns
U.S. Editor: Kara Murray

Picture credits: Sally Henry and Trevor Cook

Library of Congress Cataloging-in-Publication Data

Henry, Sally.
  Painting / Sally Henry.
      p. cm. — (Make your own art)
  Includes index.
  ISBN 978-1-4358-2511-6 (library binding)
  ISBN 978-1-4358-2644-1 (pbk)
  ISBN 978-1-4358-2656-4 (6-pack)
  1.  Painting—Technique—Juvenile literature.  I. Title.
  ND1146.H46 2009
  751.4—dc22
                              2008011133


Manufactured in China

# Contents

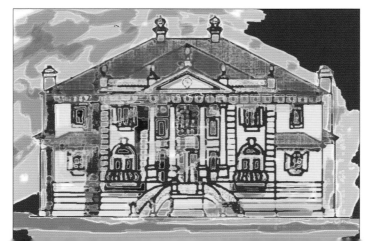

# Introduction

This book contains a number of activities to help improve your skills at painting. You can begin with something observed or completely imaginary. The object is to produce something that you can be proud of and be pleased to keep and display.

## Paper

We usually paint on white or colored paper or card stock. Most of the activities in this book have been done on heavy **drawing paper**. This is strong paper that can be used for drawing or painting. One advantage of paper over heavier materials is that you can easily cut your picture to the best shape and size when you've finished.

## Drawing board

You will need something to support your paper while you work. Your paper may come in a pad, which may have a stiff back, but using a drawing board is much better. A piece of plywood about 24 x 16 inches (60 x 40 cm) will do. Make sure it's flat. This is big enough for an 11 x 17-inch (279 x 432 mm) piece of paper. Use sticky tape to hold the paper in place on the board. Leaving a border unpainted around your painting will help it to stay flat. You can cut out your painting when you've finished.

# Paint

We've used **poster paints** and **ready-mixed paints** in the activities in the book. They can be used thick or thin and colors can be mixed. You can make the paint thinner by adding water. You can buy different containers and mixing palettes. We like mixing our paint on old white plates and having water in yogurt containers!

# Brushes

**Brushes** can be expensive, so it's very important to try as many as you can before you buy your own. In the directions we suggest some ideal sizes, but mostly you are going to need one brush for painting large areas of color and another for detail work. Soft brushes are best with the paint we are going to use.

round brushes

Some brushes are designed for special jobs. You might find you like using them in your painting. The **lettering brush** is designed for drawing letters neatly, but it also makes some interesting marks. The **blending brush** is used dry to blend areas of wet color into each other.

flat brush

blending brush

lettering brush

# Color

It's possible to get very good results with just a few basic colors. Here's a group of colors mixed from only six colors – magenta, yellow, cyan, red, green and blue. Keep your paints clean when you mix colors. Always wash your brush when you change colors.

Adding white to your color makes a **tint**.

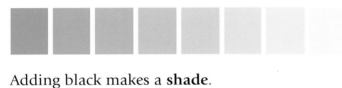

Adding black makes a **shade**.

We can use this to get the effect of light shining on something.

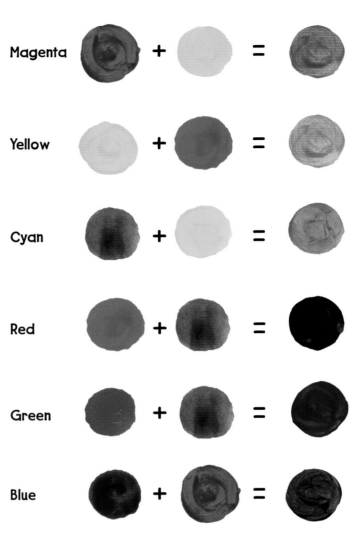

Magenta + = 

Yellow + = 

Cyan + = 

Red + = 

Green + = 

Blue + = 

# Aerial perspective

When we look into the distance, especially when there is moisture in the air, colors appear paler and more blue the further away they are. This is useful to show depth in a landscape.

6

# Linear perspective

Where there are straight lines in the landscape, such as on buildings, roads or railroad tracks, following a few simple rules will help your picture to be more realistic. Make a vanishing point in your picture. Things going directly away from you will disappear into the distance at this point.

# Framing the view

Make one of these handy tools to help you compose your picture.
• A piece of cardboard with a rectangular hole in it about 7 x 5 inches (18 x 13 cm).

# Tracing

If you've copied a picture by tracing it using tracing paper, you might need to transfer the drawing to another piece of paper. Turn the tracing over and rub soft pencil over where the drawing is. Place the tracing, right side up, on the new paper and draw over all the lines. This will transfer the drawing onto the paper.

# Take care of your work

Always take care of your work. Finishing painting and cleaning up must include making your work safe for next time or keeping your finished paintings safe. Keep your flat artwork in a folder—you can easily make one from two sheets of cardboard and some duct tape, like the one on the right.

cardboard

duct tape

flaps

# Self-Portrait

Painting a good self-portrait is a skill that takes lots of practice. Let's be our own model!

**45** MINUTES

**10** MINUTES

## You will need:

- Drawing paper
- Paints and mixing palette
- Brushes, round ⅛ and ¼ inch and flat ½ inch (3, 6, and 12 mm)
- Wall or table mirror
- Chair or stool

## What to do...

Make sure your mirror is firmly fixed and in the right place. Sit in front of the mirror with your board so you can comfortably see both your reflection and your drawing without moving your head. Is there enough light?

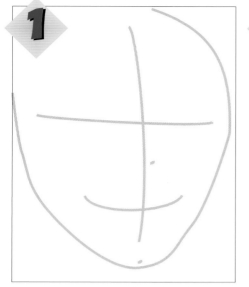

Lightly draw the shape of your head. Halfway down, draw a guideline for your eyes, then one for your mouth. Put in a center line. Put dots for the tip of your nose and your chin.

Mix up some thick paint to make a skin color. Using a ¼-inch (6 mm) brush, paint in the shapes of your eyes, mouth, nose, face and neck. Look very carefully at your eyes in the mirror.

Using your small brush, paint in your eye color. Put black dots in the center for the pupils. A tiny white highlight dot will make your eyes look more lifelike.

Paint your skin color in three shades. Touch in your lips, then use a bigger brush to paint your hair. Add hair colors: dark first, then texture with lighter colors.

Add detail to your mouth and teeth. Use dark color for eyebrows and eyelashes. Be careful – you can change the look on your face with these!

Check details and clean up. Good job. It's finished!

# Simple Still Life

Painters through the ages have used still lifes to show off lots of different ways of painting. Here we are using it to experiment with color.

**35 MINUTES**

**10 MINUTES**

## You will need:

- *Drawing paper*
- *Soft pencil, ruler*
- *Paints, mixing palette and water*
- *Brushes, ¼, ½ and 1 inch (6, 12, and 25 mm)*
- *Objects to make an arrangement*

## What to do...

Set up your group of objects in a good light. We've chosen plain backgrounds and strong colors for our first still life. Use your viewfinder frame to check your composition. Place your paper so that you can work and look directly at your group of objects. Draw a large square on your paper in pencil to mark out the shape of your painting.

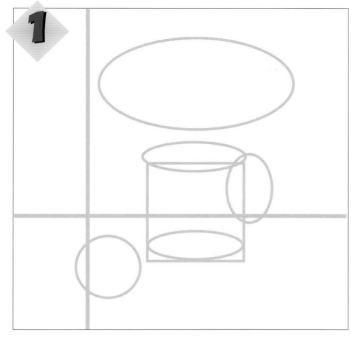

Our composition seems to fit well on a square shape. Place the objects in the painting using simple outlines only.

We are using the edges of our window to make a big L-shape in the background. It helps to frame our arrangement. Next, we draw in the flowers and the jug.

This picture is all flat shapes, but we can use the outline to describe the different things in it. Paint the table, wall and window with flat colors.

Keep your edges sharp and colors clear.
A little extra detail added to the flowers among all the flat shapes gives the picture a center.

# My Own Room

**45 MINUTES**

**10 MINUTES**

When you make a painting of your own room, you're free to put in all the things that are important to you, and to leave out everything that's dull and boring. If you want to change the decor, here's a way of trying new colors without making a big mess!

## You will need:

- *Drawing paper, soft pencil*
- *Ruler*
- *Paints, mixing palette and water*
- *Brushes, ¼, ½ and 1 inch*
  *(6, 12 and 25 mm)*

## What to do...

Think about the shape of your room. What would you see if you took away one wall and looked inside? First, draw the box shape you'd have if there wasn't any furniture in the room at all.

Outline three or four of the important things in your room. We chose the bed, the dresser, the rug and the picture.

In your painting, try putting different colors on the walls, floor and ceiling.

Notice how strong colors change the room. Dark walls can make the room feel smaller.

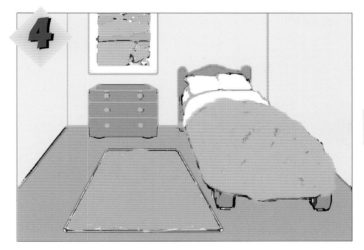

Light-colored walls can make your room seem bigger.

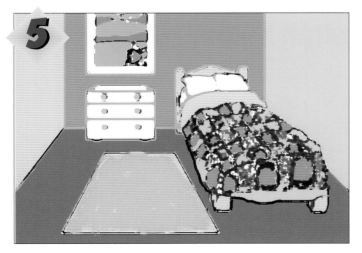

Reds and yellows make the room feel warmer.

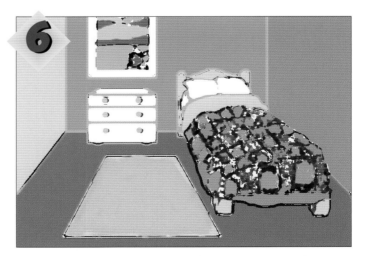

Greens and blues give the room a colder feel.

# Landscape

**40 MINUTES**

**10 MINUTES**

A landscape is all about what you can see outdoors, but that doesn't have to mean the countryside. A town or city view can be just as interesting to a painter. You can find natural scenes to paint in parks and gardens.

## You will need:

- Card stock or paper, tissues
- Paint, mixing palette and water
- Brushes, round ⅛ and ¼ inch and flat ½ inch (3, 6, and 12 mm)
- Cardboard to make a framing window

## What to do...

Find a view that interests you. You may start from a photograph, but it's often more interesting to start with the real thing. You can choose a viewpoint you really like. Use the framing window to find a good composition in the landscape. We chose our view for its bright colors and surprising patterns.

Look carefully at your composition. Try to see the pattern in the landscape. Sometimes it helps to squint your eyes to blur the view so you can't see detail. Outline the spots of color with light gray paint and a fine brush. Paint in key details, such as trees.

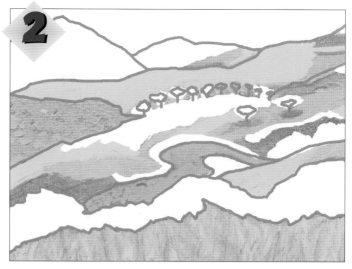

Start filling in the shapes. Do the light colors first. Don't worry about painting over your drawing lines. You can give a feeling of depth by making colors more washed out towards the horizon. Build up the trees and bushes with light and dark greens.

Use light blue to create the sky. Add darker blue as needed. If your sky has clouds, you can leave the paper unpainted to show up as white shapes. Paint landscapes in settled weather conditions to avoid having the light change.

Our picture was done in the early evening when the hills looked very pink. Add darker colors last, to show shadows under trees, for example. Make a note of where and when you made the painting.

# Dinosaur

Use a toy dinosaur for a model. Get up close to one of nature's most terrifying animals.

## You will need:

- *Model dinosaur*
- *Pencil, colored markers*
- *Drawing paper*
- *Paints, brushes and water*

**20 MINUTES**

## What to do...

Position your model dinosaur against a plain background. We used a T. rex, but you can use any models you have at home.

**5 MINUTES**

Here is a photo of our model. There's lots of detail. We can choose which parts to paint.

Make a pencil drawing of the head. Check the angle by looking at your model. Draw in his teeth, then carefully position his eye.

Use a black marker to draw over your pencil lines and make textures.

Use paint to fill in the background. We used blues and greens for the land, but you can try out wilder colors in your paintings.

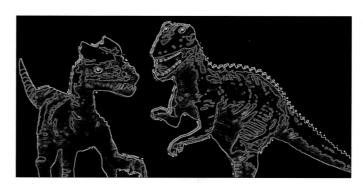

# Figure Painting

**35 MINUTES**

**10 MINUTES**

Painting figures takes lots of practice. To help you improve your skills, first try using a photograph as a basis for your painting. You may find that you need to paint details like hands by looking at real ones.

## You will need:

- Card stock or paper, tracing paper
- Drawing board, soft pencil
- Tape or thumbtacks, tissues
- Paints, mixing palette and water
- Brushes, round ⅛ and ¼ inch and flat ½ inch (3, 6 and 12 mm)

## What to do...

Try to find a large photograph to make a tracing for a painting of the same size. Otherwise you could scale your picture as described on page 26.

Select the part of the picture you want to use. Here we are going to leave out the boy on the right.

Tape tracing paper over the photo and make a detailed line drawing in pencil. Make sure to include as much detail as you can.

Cover the back of the tracing with soft pencil. Transfer the image to your drawing paper.

Using paint mixed with lots of water, lay pale color washes over your drawing.

Study your photo to find more details to add.

Paint in shadows, skin tones and more detail.

# Creatures

All sorts of creatures bring colour into our world. Let's celebrate our favorite animal by making a painting.

**35 MINUTES**

**10 MINUTES**

## You will need:

- *Drawing paper or thin card stock*
- *Paper varnish*
- *Black markers, soft pencil*
- *Paint, mixing palette and water*
- *Brushes, round ⅛ and ¼ inch and flat ½ inch (3, 6 and 12 mm)*
- *Magazines, scissors*

## What to do...

Find a photograph of an animal or bird on which you can draw. For our picture, we've chosen to paint just the macaw's head and body. We are using the top half of our photo. You can cut your reference picture to improve the design of your painting. Always ask an adult to help you when you are using scissors. Draw a grid of squares on your photo.

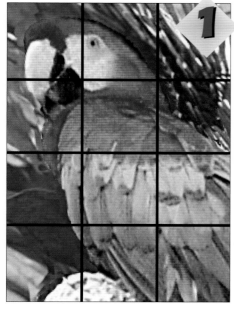

Our photo divides neatly into four squares one way and three squares the other.

On the painting paper, draw similar squares, but they can be bigger to fit the paper. Now we can start drawing. Begin with the outline.

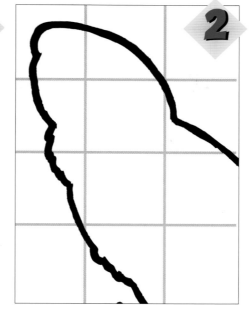

Next, use a finer pen to draw in all the smaller shapes. Be careful to put the eye in the right place.

Once you have drawn around all the different-colored feathers, you can start coloring them.

If your model is brightly colored like our macaw parrot, you need to keep your colors clear and bright, too! Finish off with some clear paper varnish.

## If you have a pet...

Make a big drawing of it in marker, then paint it!

# Pop Art Posters

**55 MINUTES**

**5 MINUTES**

Portraits are often painted in realistic colors, but you can also go wild! See what you can do!

## You will need:

- *Card stock, paper, tracing paper, tissues*
- *Black markers, soft pencil, photocopier*
- *Magazine pictures or a photograph*
- *Black wax crayon, paints, brushes and water*

## What to do...

You could work with a model for this project. Otherwise use a photo or magazine picture. Try to get 11 x 17-inch (279 x 432 mm) photocopies to paint. The four pictures together will look great.

Make a line drawing or tracing from a good photograph.

Outline the features, hair and some details of clothing.

Make four big photocopies and paint in the areas with color.

Purple, orange and green are unlikely but interesting!

Blue, green and purple are cool colors to use.

Green, yellow and pink gives an unearthly look!

Make a line drawing from a photograph or from a model. Transfer your drawing to four separate sheets of paper by tracing (see page 7) or by using a photocopier.

Use a black wax crayon to draw over the outlines on each copy. Try to follow your original lines, but don't worry if they are not all the same.

Color the four pictures differently, as on page 24. The wax crayon will repel the paint and make it easy to color in. Differences in the drawings will add interest.

These are some of the warm colors we used.

# House of Wax

Painting buildings is a challenge. We've chosen to paint one looking straight ahead, with plenty of detail but without very much depth. We have scaled the drawing from a small reference picture and used wax on dark paper. Are you ready to give it a try?

## You will need:

**40 MINUTES**

- *Dark-colored paper*
- *Drawing pad or board*
- *Tape or thumbtacks, tissues*
- *White pencil, ruler*
- *Paints and mixing palette*
- *Brushes, round ⅛ and ¼ inch and flat ½ inch (3, 6 and 12 mm)*
- *Photocopy of reference picture*
- *Wax candle*
- *Liquid soap*

## What to do...

**10 MINUTES**

Use a photocopy of your picture. Fix your dark paper to your drawing board. Follow the steps to create the grids. Move from square to square transferring the main lines in the building from the reference to your work. Experiment with wax and paint mixed with ordinary liquid soap to get great texture effects.

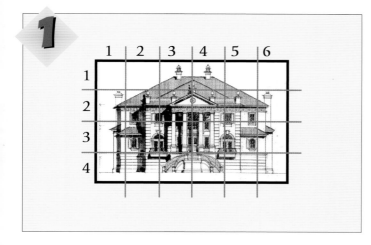

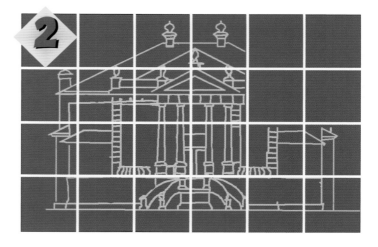

Use a photocopy reference smaller than your work. Draw a grid of squares on the reference.

Draw the same number of squares, but larger, on your paper. Draw lightly in white pencil.

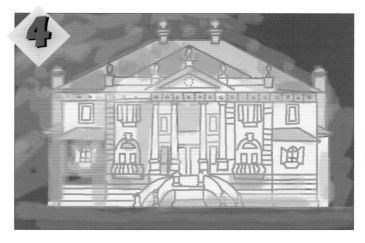

27

In each square, copy the outlines in gray paint. When dry, draw over the outlines with a candle.

Paint your house with thinned paint. The color should run off the waxy lines.

Mixing liquid soap with your paint produces interesting effects.

We've filled in the sky with blue, but you can leave it as the dark-paper color if you prefer.

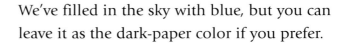

# Magic Palace

We've painted an imaginary palace, full of color, with an exotic garden. Follow our way of building up a painting or create your own in a similar way.

The magic palace painting is full of busy patterns. Look at the blown-up details in color. We have made simple line drawings of the patterns.

Before you start your own magic palace, try drawing some patterns. Paint them in with colors you like. This is

the time to experiment. When you find a set of colors that look good together, keep them for your next painting.

To add to the textures, we

have often painted over dry color with more detail. You can do this too. We also used a fine

metallic gold marker to outline some parts of the painting. It

gives it a really rich look. By freely experimenting, you can create your own effects.

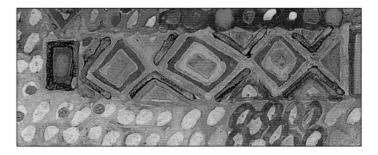

Plan your painting by doing a line drawing of your palace.

Using another color, draw in some plants in the garden and some people.

Paint in the background of the painting. Use flat colors to fill in the shapes you've drawn.

Add further interest to the picture by putting in more and more detail and texture. It's lots of fun.

# Glossary

drawing board

**backgrounds**     (BAK-growndz)  The parts of pictures that are behind the other parts.

**blending**     (BLEND-ing)  Mixing together completely.

**contains**     (kun-TAYNZ)  Holds.

**depth**     (DEPTH)  How deep something is or looks.

**designed**     (dih-ZYNZD)  Planned the form of something.

**drawing board**     (DRAW-ing BAWRD)  A flat piece of plywood or something similar for supporting  drawing paper.

**linear**     (LIH-nee-ur)  The kind of perspective in which lines converge at the vanishing point.

**materials**     (muh-TEER-ee-ulz)  What something is made of.

**palette**     (PA-lit)  This is a tray or board that you mix paints on. It can also mean the range of colors that you are using.

**rectangular**     (rek-TAN-gyoo-lur)  Like a square but longer one way than the other.

**self- portrait**     (self-POR-tret)  A picture done by the artist of himself or herself.

**texture**     (TEKS-chur)  How something feels, or looks like it might feel, when you touch it.

**tracing paper**     (TRAYS-ing PAY-per)  Thin but strong paper you can see through. Put it on top of something you want to copy and draw on it.

**varnish**     (VAHR-nish)  A liquid, usually clear, for brushing onto finished oil paintings. Paper varnish is also available for drawings.

# Index

# Web Sites

Due to the changing nature of Internet links, PowerKids Press has developed an online list of Web sites related to the subject of this book. This site is updated regularly. Please use this link to access the list:
www.powerkidslinks.com/myoa/paint